The Little Book of

BIG

IDEAS

✳

The Little Book of

BIG

IDEAS

**INSPIRATION, ENCOURAGEMENT,
AND TIPS TO STIMULATE CREATIVITY
AND IMPROVE YOUR LIFE**

Harold R. McAlindon

FOREWORD BY MICHAEL MICHALKO
Author of *Thinkertoys*

Cumberland House
Nashville, Tennessee

Published by Cumberland House Publishing, 431 Harding Industrial Drive, Nashville, Tennessee 37211-3160.

Cover design by Bruce Gore, Gore Studio, Inc.
Text design by Mary Sanford.

Library of Congress Cataloging-in-Publication Data
McAlindon, Harold R., 1940-
    The little book of big ideas : inspiration, encouragement, and tips to stimulate creativity and improve your life / [written and compiled by] Harold R. McAlindon ; foreword by Michael Michalko.
      p.   cm.
    ISBN 1-58182-054-2 (pbk. : alk. paper)
    1. Conduct of life Quotations, maxims, etc. 2. Creative ability Quotations, maxims, etc. 3. Creative thinking Quotations, maxims, etc.   I. Title.   II. Title: Big Ideas.
PN6084.C556M33   1999
646.7--dc21   99-44288
                                        CIP

Printed in the United States of America
1 2 3 4 5 6 7 8—04 03 02 01 00 99

Ideas are the fuel of progress and foundation of our future. This book is dedicated to those individuals and organizations that nurture and reward creativity.

HOW TO USE THIS BOOK

This book is intended to be a creative friend. Skim it, write in it, and highlight important passages. Periodically review it for insight or encouragement. Add your own thoughts and ideas. The main thing is to use it as mental nutrition and motivation. Keep feeding and acting upon your creative impulses. Wonderful things will happen.

CONTENTS

FOREWORD

Creativity is the spark that ignites success, and top companies and organizations are embracing it passionately around the world. Creativity abounds at ever-fertile 3M, which annually introduces hundreds of new products. It's the driving force behind Pfizer, which introduces a steady stream of top-of-the line drugs out of their labs to the market each year. It's what made Enron into a very different kind of power company, and what made Mirage Resorts a dazzling success in the gambling casino business. Even Coca-Cola, whose financial success has been predicated on a single unvarying product for more than a century, has become relentlessly creative in recent years.

To these and many other of the world's top companies and organizations, creativity isn't frizzy-haired scientists in white coats or long-haired artistic types staring into space, but rather a belief in and reverence for creativity that permeates the whole organization from top to bottom. It's in their staffing, strategy, new product development, branding, marketing, distribution, pricing, and business processes. Creativity is, literally, in every aspect of their business and is a distinctive style of their corporate behavior that's comfortable with new ideas, change, risk, and failure.

Creativity is within everyone's reach. Get it right and you can dramatically change your company and your life.

Virtually all companies with high marks in creativity have had a significant impact on their industry and, in the process, produced impressive increases in earnings and market capitalization. For example, a little over ten years ago, Enron, a gas utility, was losing money. Today it is highly profitable, and its stock has quadrupled over that period. How did Enron do it? Not by being a traditionally run, conventional gas utility and not by doing things the way they were always done. They did it with one single new idea that changed their entire industry.

In the late 1980s, Kenneth Lay was at Enron, which had just been formed by the merger of two natural gas giants. Lay figured it was a good opportunity to look at the industry in a different way. At the time, government regulation required a gas pipeline to run single-mindedly from a specific field to a specific utility company, with few shifts or diversions. A map of all the natural gas lines looks like a vast cobweb of interconnections criss-crossing multiple times.

Lay viewed the national network of gas pipelines differently than just about everybody. He saw it as a unique, interconnected, distribution system capable of shipping gas from any gas field to any local gas company, rather than as lines running from specific fields directly to particular gas companies. He recognized that by pushing deregulation, Enron could use all those natural gas lines as a network to buy gas where it was cheap and ship it to where it was needed. So, while other gas companies were vigorously resisting deregulation, Enron hired aggressive, well-compensated traders and single-handedly created spot markets in gas when the industry was deregulated. To accelerate rapid growth, Enron also created new public companies, majority-owned by Enron.

The traditional companies were convinced that there was no need for a spot market approach and no need to change the way they did business. While they passively watched, Enron proved that its new approach and creative new structure could reduce the cost of gas for some utilities by 30 to 50 percent. Kenneth Lay's idea changed the concept of how the natural gas industry was run and created new products, new services, new kinds of contracts, and new ways of pricing.

With the cost of free-market gas so cheap as a result of the spot market approach, Lay even thought the unthinkable: using gas for fuel in electric generation plants. Consequently, Enron built and operated its own gas-fired power plant in Texas and demonstrated that it could compete economically against coal-fired plants, with far less pollution. Incredibly, Lay created a huge, new market for natural gas as fuel for electric generations, a fuel that benefits us all by reducing the amount of pollution in the atmosphere.

Gadgets, patents, new inventions, R&D, breakthrough technologies, luck? At Enron, not a one. By thinking creatively, Kenneth Lay looked at the same information as everyone else and saw something different. His single idea about a spot market approach to fuel turned Enron into the most innovative power company in the country and changed the nature of an entire industry.

Kenneth Lay's example is one of a multiplicity of

examples of the impact of a single idea or thought. Breakthrough ideas are within the reach of all us, but many of us have forgotten how to look for them. There is an ancient Chinese story about a rainmaker who was hired to bring rain to a parched part of China. The rainmaker came in a covered cart, a small, wizened, old man who sniffed the air with obvious disgust as he got out of his cart, and asked to be left alone in a cottage outside the village; even his meals were to be left outside the door.

Nothing was heard from him for three days, then it not only rained, but there was a big downfall of snow, unknown at that time of year. Very much impressed, the villagers sought him out and asked how he could make it rain, and even snow. The rainmaker replied, "I have not made the rain or the snow; I am not responsible for it." The villagers insisted that they had been in the midst of a terrible drought until he came, and then after three days they even had quantities of snow.

"Oh, I can explain that. You see, the rain and snow were always here. But as soon as I got here, I saw that the people did not know how to look. So I remained here until you could see what was always right here before your eyes."

Harold McAlindon's wonderful *The Little Book of Big Ideas* is filled with tips on how to stimulate your creativity and improve your life. It will inspire and motivate you to look for and find the ideas that are always right before your eyes.

MICHAEL MICHALKO

INTRODUCTION

This book was written for men and women who desire to turn ideas into bank deposits and dreams into reality. There are millions of great ideas in the world waiting for us to use them. We must dedicate our minds, hearts, spirits, eyes, ears, arms, and legs to putting these ideas into action. The supply of ideas is inexhaustible. Let a great idea use you. Stand up for it. Work for it. Teach it. Sell it. Crusade for it. Help make it become a reality through you.

Creating something worthwhile and of value can be a lot of fun. It will also be a lot of work. We all occasionally need a jump start, support, or a kick in the pants. This book is intended to provide all three. Our creative and innovative capacities must be nurtured and harnessed if we are to live up to our ultimate potential. I hope this book provides some of that encouragement and stimulation.

HAROLD R. MCALINDON

The Little Book of

BIG

IDEAS

✸

1

stirring your creative juices

WHAT IS A BIG IDEA?

Big ideas come in all shapes and sizes. To recognize them we have to be searching for them and be open to their power.

A big idea changes your life. It helps solve a problem, create opportunity, or enriches your life in ways that are important to you.

My method for identifying big ideas is not very scientific. A big idea will excite you. It puts a spring in your step and a sparkle in your eye. It will stir your creative juices and demand that you pursue it with passion.

Finally, it is an idea that is truly you, unique to your interests, talents and ambitions. I hope this book will help you discover yours!

Progress begins with an individual idea. Quality thoughts precede quality results. Mental stimulation is an individual thing. Creative men and women of all ages had unique approaches and philosophies about tapping into their creative potential. Think about the insights on the following pages and find yours. Nurture it and use it! The world needs it!

CREATIVE REFLECTIONS

Actualizing your creative potential is promoted with a relaxed introspection of yourself.

What makes me happy?
Who makes me happy?
What am I proud of?
What is really important to me?
How am I spending my life?
What am I contributing?
What do I believe in?
Who do I believe in?
What do I stand for?
Am I living up to my potential?
What are my strengths?
What are my values?

Creativity, when not used, turns to depression.

— HENRI REIMAN

Clarity of mind, body and spirit is the key to creativity.

— DAN WAKEFIELD

Assumptions are the death of possibilities.

— JAMES MAPES

Plant as many positive seeds as you can. Your positive harvest will be great.

All great accomplishments begin with the germ of an idea in the mind of a creative individual.

Practice seeing things from perspectives other than your own.

PERSONAL BENEFITS TO CREATIVITY

There are many reasons why an idea rich life is a worthy pursuit. The following are a few of the most valuable personal gains.

1. An intense "aliveness" and increased self-confidence.
2. Reduction of stress.
3. An inner sense of well being and peace.
4. More control of your job and your life.
5. Personal satisfaction of experiencing your true self in unique and fulfilling ways

Creativity is a rare part of living. It's fundamental. None of us can squelch our creativity without feeling less than whole, incomplete and depressed.

— Lynn Weiss, Ph.D.

Creative inspiration is all around us. We must be open to it. Ideas can be spawned by:

- A warm bath
- Solitude
- Music
- A joke
- Children
- Nature
- A walk
- Inner reflection
- Writing
- Movies
- A sunrise or a sunset
- Books
- Conversation with friends
- Senior citizens

LOOKING WITHIN

What are my interests?

What are my strengths?

What is unique about me ?

What do I love?

What are my passions?

Who can I help?

What makes me happy?

What do I value?

What do I want to accomplish?

What do I want to contribute?

How do I define "Success"?

Generate as many ideas as you can because ultimately quantity breeds quality.

Follow what you love and it will take you where you want to go.

— NATALIE GOLDBERG

Pursue your passion and live your dream.

As you nurture your own creativity, life will naturally become more meaningful, satisfying, and enjoyable.

The place you are in needs you today.

— KATHERINE LOGAN

How to Generate Ideas

Dr. Arthur Van Gundy lists these three "musts" for generating a lot of quality ideas:

1. People must have a belief that anything is possible. Thinking outside the box makes idea generation limitless.

2. A climate is needed that is conducive to creative thinking. People need to be encouraged, and ideas need a safe place to be born and nurtured.

3. People need lots of different stimuli, which are both related and unrelated to the challenge. This triggers new associations and encourages creativity.

The greatest discovery of our age is that people can alter their reality by altering their states of mind.

— WILLIAM JAMES

Your creativity comes from within you, not from without.

Honor your creative nature.

A variety of interests in life will help you grow creatively.

To create is to touch the spirit.

— MICHELL CASSON AND STEWART CURLEY

Choose, or create, a profession that "turns you on."

When your interest is sparked, follow it!

The mind needs exercise as much as the body does.

— JOHN MORGAN

Do not wish to be anything but what you are, and try to be that perfectly.

— SAINT FRANCIS DE SALES

Pay attention to what you tell yourself.

Your words create what you speak about. Learn to speak positively.

— SANATA ROMAN

Each of us possesses a creative self. Claiming that is a transformational art. When you begin to act on your creativity, what you find inside may be more valuable than what you produce for the external world. The ultimate creative act is to express what is most authentic and individual about you.

— EILEEN M. CLEGG

Research shows that 90 percent of five-year olds are creative, but only 2 percent of adults are.

— LEE SILBER

We are all capable of much more than we think we are.

Your reality is under your control.

Doubting your doubts removes the imaginary obstacles that we construct.

Say YES to ideas, challenges, and life.

Music has the capacity to touch the innermost reaches of the soul and music gives flight to the imagination.

— PLATO

Find your strength, develop a positive attitude, and commit yourself to excellence. This is a sure path to success.

That the mind has great power over the body, there is not the slightest doubt.

Everything you need for a happy life is within yourself.

Consciously make your attitudes work for you.

We grow by dealing with new ideas, new people, new experiences.

⤙ Dr. Oakley Ray

All of us can create if we allow ourselves to.

⤙ Natalie Goldberg

To thine own self, be the true you.

⤙ Eureka Truth

Most folks will be as happy as they make up their minds to be.

⤙ Abraham Lincoln

The environment you fashion out of your thoughts, your beliefs, your ideals, your philosophy is the environment you live in.

Your mind is formed from the inside out.

Everyone is born creative.

The less money you require, the more career options you have.

It is better to create than to be learned; creating is the true essence of life.

— NIEBUHR

Take charge of your thoughts.

— PLATO

Having completed a task means having become eternal.

— LAO TZU

You are probably ten times more creative than you realize.

— BEVERLY MOORE

A positive attitude is a person's ticket to a better future.

Find your creative intersection where your talents, skills and interests overlap.

You are the only one that can do what only you can do.

Creative thought requires a clear head— take a good brain shower.

— DR. MORTIMER ADLER

Stereotypes about creativity have been proven wrong.

The visions that we present our children shape the future.

We become what we think about.

To find your creativity you must search for it.

We are born optimists. That's why babies smile.

— RICHARD GAYLORD BRILEY

As you nurture your own creativity, life will naturally become more meaningful, satisfying and enjoyable.

Many of our best ideas come from our subconscious.

Creativity is within everyone.

— RENE MCPHERSON

Intuition, will, joy, strength, and compassion—these qualities of essence form your creative base.

— ROCHELLE MYERS

According to the Johnson O'Connor Foundation, 702 tests of women showed them to be as much as 25 percent ahead of men in relative creativity.

↝ *YOUR CREATIVE POWER*

Experience takes away more than it adds.

↝ PLATO

Be self loving. It enables you to love others.

Think of creativity as a long-term relationship.

Keep feeding your mind.

Creativity is an expression of who we are, not what we do or have.

Creativity is the urge to express our "aliveness."

Trust your instincts.

Create a reputation for being imaginative.

There are many more people trying to meet the right person than trying to become the right person.

We don't try to be 100 percent better, rather 1 percent better a hundred ways.

— ANN MITCHELL

The best way to begin the creative process is with a blank sheet of paper.

The best way to learn to create is by creating. Practice is always more important than theory.

When your life itself becomes the subject matter of the creative process, a very different experience of life opens to you.

— ROBERT FRITZ

There are ideas in your mind waiting to come into the world.

A creative attitude is the fuel of progress and growth. Stay mentally young. Keep dreaming.

The creative brain is triggered by the senses (sight, smell, taste, touch, and sound).

Good ideas don't work unless we do.

The fear of rejection can paralyze creative thinking.

Remember you're a creative person not a corporate lawyer or investment broker.

Most depression arises from erroneous thinking.

—DR. DAVID D. BURNS

Imagination is the beginning of creation. We imagine what we desire; we will what we imagine; and at last we create what we will.

—GEORGE BERNARD SHAW

CREATIVE ACTIONS

1. What areas of your life would you like to change or improve?
2. Put your creative goals in writing and carry them with you.
3. Every day conciously change one of your habits.
4. Make a habit of generating ideas.
5. Look for a creative use for some common product.

2

humor is serious business

The relationship between humor and creativity is not surprising. The punch line of a joke is "funny" because it takes an unexpected twist or turn. Some of our best ideas surface because we make unusual associations, combinations, or applications of information. When we are happy, in a good mood, and having fun, the prospects of coming up with a creative gem skyrocket.

Laughter is the best creative medicine.

— JOHN CLEESE

It is useless to close your door to new ideas, they'll come in though the window and down the chimney.

— COUNT METTERNICH

Beyond the needs of society, another significant development in the creativity movement is the realization of how vital creative thought is to an individual's psychological health.

⚊— EUGENE RAUDSEPP

An environment of playfulness and humor is highly conducive to creativity.

⚊— MICHAEL MICHALKO

Fun is fundamental.

⚊— DOUG HALL

A lot of what we think of as neurosis in this country is simply people who are unhappy because they're not using their creative resources.

⚊— JULIA CAMERON

Keep the child in you alive and keep playing.

↜ Leo Buscaglia

Over 50 percent of an illness is emotionally induced. It is by trying to meet adult problems with childish reactions that we generate emotional stress.

↜ John A. Schindler M.D.

Positive attitudes produce and promote positive health.

Relaxing, reducing anxiety helps get new ideas flowing.

↜ John Cleese

Creative people run best on the high-octane fuels of play and freedom.

Part of the happy day is refusing to be affected by negative thoughts.

When you are feeling good, don't ask why. Just immerse yourself in it.

Look for the humor in a negative situation.

Detach. Take a mental step back from negative situations.

Simplify. Let go of unimportant things.

The mind is as capable of producing health as it is sickness.

Studies have proven that the key to avoiding mental aging is to keep your mind active.

— PREVENTION MAGAZINE

Dr. Henry Link, and other eminent psychologists, agree that lack of creative effort is often at the bottom of mental unrest and nervous upsets.

Besides being good for your health, humor is an effective way to invite creativity.

＊ ERNIE J. ZELINSKI

Comedy and laughing will open up your thinking.

Don't try to teach a pig to sing. It is very difficult and will irritate the pig.

＊ HERB GABORA

The next time your mind wanders, follow it around for a while.

A rich sense of humor is reported to be a common thread among many outstanding inventors.

＊ *THINK OUTSIDE OF THE BOX*

God's greatest invention was the mind of a child.

Do something to nurture yourself. Do things that give you joy.

Creativity's biggest obstacle is uptight people.

— MIKE VANCE

Always start brainstorming with warm-up exercises.

When you're trying to be creative, think pleasant thoughts.

Imagination is intelligence having fun.

Humor takes us from Duh! . . . to
A-HA!

⤙ Don Lambert

You can revive creativity by
remembering to laugh frequently.

⤙ Randall Munson

Humor is an important factor to be
considered in the identification of high
potential associates.

⤙ Herb Gabora

Getting into a humorous frame of mind not only loosens you up, it enhances your creativity.

— ROGER VON OECH

To be brilliant, you have to be willing to be stupid.

We all have our own unique way of expressing our creativity.

Being around young people will keep you thinking young.

Creative seeds need time to blossom.

It's not by chance that I list having fun as my first suggestion on how to get your mind into idea condition . . . in my experience, it might be the most important one.

↜ JACK FOSTER

The best meetings and brainstorming sessions are playful and fun.

↜ BRYAN MATTIMORE

All meetings ought to start with telling funny stories or jokes to stimulate the group's creativity. Laughing makes us lose our inhibitions.

↜ C. DIANE EALY, PH.D.

Play is what I do for a living. The work comes in organizing the results of play

↜ *COMPUTER ARCHITECT*

Probably the number one clue that creativity and transformational thinking are happening is laughter. Laughter and fun free the mind from barriers and restrictions.

— JOYCE WYCOFF

There is little doubt that a playful group atmosphere is more likely to result in quality ideas than a more staid, serious environment.

— DR. ARTHUR VAN GUNDY

Positive people are more innovative and creative than negative "realists."

Anger inhibits your ability to think clearly or creatively.

He who laughs, lasts!

— MARY PETTIBONE POOLE

Patience is the art of concealing your impatience.

Laughter stimulates the heart.

It takes ignorance to do new-to-the-world ideas. Ignorance is as big a factor as courage—ignorance of how difficult whatever it is you're trying to do is to do.

— GUY KAWASAKI

Stress is the enemy of creativity.

Money won't buy happiness, but it allows one to be miserable in a nice neighborhood.

Creativity is so delicate a flower that praise tends to make it bloom.

— ALEX OSBORN

Criticism and creativity don't mix.

When corporations learn to laugh at themselves, customers will laugh with them.

— GEORGE LOIS

Creativity and innovation should be fun.

Tickle your mind.

> ⌐ LINDSEY COLLIER

Your imagination can be improved by having fun.

> ⌐ WILLIAM C. MILLER

If making money from your ideas isn't fun, you're going about it the wrong way.

> ⌐ BOB COLEMAN

The importance of laughter and humor in the workplace can't be emphasized enough.

> ⌐ MIKE VANCE & DIANE DEACON

The ability to laugh at circumstances
and ourselves is a sign of maturity.

Hardening of the attitudes is deadly.
Fight it with a sense of humor.

A sense of humor creates confidence,
courage and self-esteem.

Laughter doesn't mean that people are goofing off, but rather enjoying what they are doing.

Ha! Ha! = A-HA!

Humor is the great lubricant of teamwork.

Unable to create, we become angry, resentful, frustrated, and unhappy.

There are therapists who claim to specialize in treating creative people.

— THE GREAT AMERICAN IDEA BOOK

One can actually think oneself into a healthy and prosperous state.

Play with your ideas; thinking should be fun.

The crisis of yesterday is the joke of tomorrow.

— H. G. WELLS

CREATIVE ACTIONS

1. Make sure that you laugh out loud every day.

2. Share a joke or funny situation with someone and enjoy their smile or laughter.

3. Smile at yourself in the mirror every day.

4. Think of things and people that make you laugh . . . stay close to them.

5. See the "value" of making other people laugh and smile.

3

don't listen to the experts—be one

The people who have come closest to predicting the future are some of the science fiction writers unencumbered by elaborate research or prestigious committees, but with the courage to dream.

God himself could not sink this ship. The *Titanic* is unsinkable.

— WHITE STAR LINE

Edwin Land tried to sell his instant camera to Eastman Kodak. Kodak turned him down, and Land went off to found Polaroid Corporation.

Western Union turned down Alexander Graham Bell's offer to sell them his telephone patents for one hundred thousand dollars.

Chauncey M. Depew confessed that he warned his nephew not to invest five thousand dollars in Ford stocks because "nothing has come along to beat the horse."

Commodore Vanderbilt dismissed Westinghouse and his new air brakes for trains with the remark that "he had no time to waste on fools."

I'm sorry, Mr. Kipling, but you just don't know how to use the English language.

— EDITOR, *SAN FRANCISCO EXAMINER*
(TO RUDYARD KIPLING)

In 1881, when the New York YWCA announced typing lessons for women, vigorous protests were made on the grounds that the female constitution would break down under the strain.

In Germany, experts "proved" that if trains went at the frightful speed of fifteen miles per hour, blood would spurt from the travelers' noses and the passengers would suffocate going through tunnels.

Those who loaned Robert Fulton money for his steamboat project stipulated that their names be withheld for fear of ridicule were it known that they supported anything so "foolhardy."

Just a passing fad.

— PHIL WRIGLEY, ON THE ADVENT OF NIGHT BASEBALL

I think there is a world market for about five computers.

— THOMAS J. WATSON, IBM CHAIRMAN

Fifty political experts unanimously predict a Dewey victory over Truman.

⸺ NEWSWEEK

There are growing concerns that smoking has pharmacological effects that are of real value to smokers.

*⸺ JOSEPH CULLMAN III,
PRESIDENT OF PHILIP MORRIS*

"Experts" insisted that iron ships would not float, that they would manage more easily than wooden ships when grounding, that it would be difficult to preserve the iron bottoms from rust and that iron would deflect the compass.

Joshua Coopersmith was arrested in Boston for trying to sell stock in the telephone. "All well-informed people know it is impossible to transmit the human voice over a wire."

Scientist Simon Newcomb said in 1896 just as the success for the airplane was in the offing, "the demonstration that no combination of known substances, known forms of machinery, and known forms of forces can be united in a practical machine by which men shall fly seems to the writer as complete as it is possible for the demonstration of any physical fact to be."

When Buffington took out patents for the steel-frame skyscraper in 1888, the *Architectural News* predicted that the expansion and contraction of iron would crack all the plaster, eventually leaving only the shell.

Rock 'n' Roll was supposed to be a passing fad.

In the 1940s, Chester Carlson offered his patent on Xerography to IBM, RCA, and more than twenty other large companies, none of which perceived the magnitude of the opportunity. A small manufacturer of photographic paper named Halloid read about the invention, acquired the license, went into production and sold the international rights to an English concern named Rank Organization, then a film and entertainment company.

The first successful cast iron plan invented in the United States in 1797 was rejected by New Jersey farmers under the theory that cast iron poisoned the land and stimulated the growth of weeds.

Charles H. Duell, commissioner of the U.S. Patent Office, urged President William McKinley to abolish the patent office in 1899 because "everything that can be invented has been invented."

According to the theory of aerodynamics, the bumblebee cannot fly. This fact may be demonstrated through laboratory tests and wind tunnel experiments. The size, weight, and shape of its body, in relation to the total wing spread, make flying impossible. The bumblebee doesn't believe it and flies anyway.

America's major automobile tire companies rejected the radial design because it cost more than bias-ply tires. Michelin jumped to manufacture the higher-priced, high-quality radials. It took years for U.S. companies to catch up.

A Presidential commission appointed by Herbert Hoover in 1929 later reported to Franklin D. Roosevelt on how to plot our course through 1952. The report was in thirteen volumes prepared by fifty "researchers." The summary required 1,600 pages. Yet, there was not a word about atomoic energy, jet propulsion, antibiotics, transistors, or many other significant developments.

The World's Fair of 1939, which was dedicated to the World of Tomorrow, not only failed to suggest any of these advances, but did not even mention the idea of space travel.

Herman Kahn's opus on the year 2000 never mentioned pollution.

Nothing is gained by making an idea fight for its very life as soon as it is born. A thirty-four-year old engineer at Texas instruments named Jack Kilby developed the first integrated circuit in 1958 and received this brush-off: "Young, man, don't you realize that computers are getting bigger, not smaller?"

Steven Jobs and Steven Wozniak took their prototype personal computer to Hewlett-Packard and Atari, both of whom reported "our plates are full" and turned it down. So Jobs and Wozniak founded Apple Computer.

Dr. W. Edwards Deming took his quality concepts to the Japanese in 1950 because American companies were not interested. Today, quality is one of the most prevalent strategies being pursued by companies in the United States.

Literary works by John Grisham and Norman Vincent Peale and Margaret Mitchell's classic novel, *Gone With the Wind*, were all initially rejected by major publishers.

It was declared that the introduction of the railroad would require the building of many insane asylums as people would be driven mad with terror at the sight of locomotives rushing across the country.

CREATIVE ACTIONS

1. Ask yourself why "experts" are wrong so many times.

2. Make three predictions that you can see happening in the next twenty-five years.

3. What are experts wrong about today?

4. Who do you consider today's "real" experts?

5. What can you do to become an expert?

4

getting serious about creativity

BE READY

To every person there comes in their lifetime that special moment when you are figuratively tapped on the shoulder and offered the chance to do a very special thing, unique to you and your talents. What a tragedy if that moment finds you unprepared or unqualified for work which could have been your finest hour.

— SIR WINSTON CHURCHILL

Don't let ideas die premature deaths because they're not ready to stand alone.

THE CREATIVE THINKER'S SWEET SIXTEEN

1. Choose to live a creative life.
2. Make creativity a daily habit.
3. Capture your ideas.
4. Take intelligent risks.
5. Have fun with your ideas.
6. Be yourself.
7. Act on your creative urges.
8. Keep feeding your mind.
9. Stimulate your senses.
10. Create from your passion.
11. Take a daily step toward your dream.
12. Have an idea-friendly place to create.
13. Keep creative resources nearby.
14. Have creative companions.
15. Learn from your mistakes.
16. Never give up.

CREATIVE THINKING SECRETS

Creative thinking is very personal. Different things work for different people. The following items all seem to positively affect the creative process.

1. Make creative thinking enjoyable.
2. Enjoy a light snack or beverage while you are thinking.
3. Doodle while you think.
4. Think in a self-designed idea-friendly environment.
5. Dress comfortably.
6. Play soft music while you create.
7. Don't press yourself to create.
8. Give yourself time to warm up your creative juices.
9. Read some stimulating thoughts.
10. Do whatever else works for you.

Creativity thrives on stimulation, change, challenge, need, and adversity. Using creativity in a proactive fashion makes virtually anything possible.

What we create is an expression of our inner wishes, thoughts, and values.

Working with ideas without knowing the process is like building a car by trial and error.

Happiness lies in the joy of achievement and the thrill of creative effort.

— FRANKLIN D. ROOSEVELT

Create an idea-friendly environment for yourself. Organize to suit yourself. Surround yourself with stimulation, inspiration, and courage.

SUCCESS QUOTIENT

Candidly answer the following questions:

1. Do I have a passion for my idea?
2. Do I have the emotional makeup to withstand obstacles and keep going?
3. Do I have the resources to do it?
4. Is the support that I need available to me?
5. Is the market large enough?
6. Are there clear competitive advantages to my idea?
7. Are the obstacles that I must overcome clear to me?
8. Can I reach the market?
9. Can I reach the market in an inexpensive way?

Habits That Kill Creativity

Just as certain habits promote idea generation, others are deadly to the process. The following must be eliminated.

1. Wallowing in self-pity.
2. Failing to assume responsibility for your actions and reactions.
3. Giving up your dreams and ideals.
4. Comparing your weaknesses to others' strengths.
5. Holding grudges.
6. Being passive toward your goals.
7. Overreacting to criticism.
8. Failing to articulate positive observations.
9. Underestimating your potential.
10. Giving up.

What do your creative instincts say about your idea? Trust them.

Don't let ideas die of neglect.

Don't be your own worst enemy, be your own best friend.

Creativity is what the creative person does.

Failure is only the opportunity to begin again more intelligently.

The first step to being creative is to get rid of your own unwritten rules.

— MARY M. BYERS

Worry is the misuse of imagination.

Innovative management is a strategic weapon.

I start where the last person left off.

↞ THOMAS EDISON

I think the biggest part of creativity in medicine is listening.

↞ DR. ALEXA CANADY

Most people are ready to play the devil's advocate. Think of all the positive things that can be done with an idea. Don't quit until you can find at least ten things.

Protect ideas until they are strong enough to stand alone.

Everyone is born a genius, but the process of living degeniuses them.

— BUCKMINSTER FULLER

Develop a mental storehouse for ideas and positive thoughts.

Use your strengths in creative ways.

Before you reject an idea, find at least five good things about it.

None of my inventions came by accident. They came by work.

— THOMAS EDISON

Nothing great was ever created without enthusiasm.

— RALPH WALDO EMERSON

Focus on your success, no matter how small.

Keep looking until you find an open door. Too many good ideas die premature deaths.

Recycle your ideas. Sometimes timing determines their worth.

Slowing down is sometimes the best way to speed up.

Creativity is the making of the new and the rearranging of the old in a new way.

— MIKE VANCE

Creativity is a core part of living.

— LYNN WEISS, PH.D.

Engage, retreat. Engage, retreat. This is the way I create.

✧ RON PITKIN

The more you create, the more you can create.

Creative thinking is like any other skill. It can be improved with practice.

The best ideas are as much spiritual A-HAs as intellectual ones.

It's during idle time that ideas have a chance to recombine in new ways.

Thinking creatively can be the difference between success and failure.

Essential Ingredients to Spiritual Creativity

People—The source of ideas

Percolation—The managing of ideas

Passion—The energy of ideas

Persistence—The work ethic of ideas

Prayers—The limitless power of ideas

A good idea doesn't care who has it.

The creative moment can be nurtured or encouraged, but not forced.

Creative thinking is the most productive form of labor.

To invent, you need a goal, imagination and a pile of junk.

— THOMAS EDISON

The best way to get great ideas is to get lots of ideas and throw the bad ones away.

The answer to any problem "pre-exists."
We need to ask the right question to
reveal the answer.

Chance favors the prepared mind.

— LOUIS PASTEUR

Rules that control, rather than inform,
can kill creativity.

Make creativity a habit.

Think of an alternate use for something
everyday.

Keep adding to your mental tool kit. New information and experience bring new possibilities.

Make it a point to rid your speech and thoughts of all forms of negative self-talk.

— KARL ALBRECHT

When the world zigs . . . zag!

Thinking creatively can be the difference between success and failure.

Abraham Maslow has stated that "we see all problems as a nail if our only tool is a hammer." We need to keep adding to our mental tool kit.

Add:
- New experiences
- More education
- Additional information
- New perspectives

    Change:
    - Routines
    - Habits
    - Roles

        Also:
        - Network
        - Meet new people
        - Reverse responsibilities

If you want a golden rule that will fit everybody, this is it: have nothing in your houses that you do not know to be useful or believe to be beautiful.

— WILLIAM MORRIS

Ideas are like rabbits. You get a couple and learn how to handle them, and pretty soon you have a dozen.

— JOHN STEINBECK

Solitude often generates powerful ideas.

Small innovations produce big results.

Work on your idea until it is so good it can't be ignored.

There are many things in life that will catch your eye, but only a few will catch your heart. Pursue these.

— UNKNOWN

CREATIVE ACTIONS

1. Every day, say to yourself "I am creative."

2. "Use" your creative abilities every day.

3. Tell others that you are making a commitment to a creative life style.

4. On your job, ask yourself, "Is there a more creative way to do this?"

5. At the end of the day, reflect on creative actions that you took since you woke up.

5

creative success is
a team sport

CREATIVE COLLABORATION

Turning ideas into reality is a team sport.
Whether your idea is a product, a book,
a business, or a service, you need the
help of other people to make it happen.
A vital key to creative success is the
practice of building on your strength and
integrating your talent with the unique
abilities of others. A creative network is
one of the most powerful engines for
driving social and economical progress.

Be the kind of person that people can
come to with their dreams, ideas, and
visions.

Creative people often don't need to be managed, they need to be inspired with a lofty vision.

Rarely does one person have the "whole best idea." Whether it is a problem or an opportunity that we are dealing with, we must integrate the fractions of ideas from many people to come up with the best end result.

Never doubt that a small group of thoughtful, courageous, creative people can change the world.

Individuals say "I," teams say "We."

A team is much more than a group of individuals.

Shared values are the unifying force of a team.

Team pride elevates creative thought.

Team spirit is a competitive advantage.

Teams can accomplish what an individual cannot.

Teams provide what you reward.

Believe in your team.

Teams turn ideas into achievement.

No one has a patent on good ideas.

Teamwork is basically cooperation and mutual respect. Be the kind of team member that would be missed.

A creative team is like an insurance policy for future success.

Teams convert ideas into bank deposits and positive change.

Diversity stimulates creativity and innovation.

None of us is as smart as all of us.

 ⌁ Ken Blanchard

Innovation creates opportunity, quality creates demand, but it takes teamwork to make it happen.

You can dream, create, design, and build the most wonderful place in the world . . . but it requires people to make the dream come to a reality.

— WALT DISNEY

Historians are increasingly sharing that even legendary "solitary" inventors really worked in groups.

Creativity is mobile. You either carry it with you or you don't have it.

The key question is not "what can we create?" or even "what do we want to create?" Rather for all of us it is "what are we called to create?"

— WILLIAM C. MILLER

The strong urge to accomplish something notable is the mainspring of nearly all creative endeavors.

Don't let your dream or vision die because of a lack of sustained effort.

Create an "idea-safe environment" for thinking.

CREATIVE TRAILBLAZERS

Pioneers and creative thinkers have common traits:

1. They have a dream.
2. They believe that the future can be different, and better.
3. They make a commitment to shape some portion of that tomorrow.
4. They look at risk in terms of opportunity and potential gains.
5. They work hard as part of a team that builds on strengths.
6. They make total investments in their goals.
7. They are minorities that create a better future for the majority.

KEEPING THE IDEA ALIVE

In a relaxed fashion, visualize your idea in its final form. See yourself and others benefiting from your creative success. Doing this for a few minutes at bedtime is a great way to condition your subconscious to work on it while you sleep. When you wake up, jot down any ideas or flashes that come to you.

There are many "reasons" for failure, but very few "excuses" that are not self-imposed.

Sometimes you need more confidence than the facts dictate.

What experts say is not as important as what leaders or fellow innovators have to say. As the great basketball coach Jon Wooden has said "those who say it can't be done should not get in the way of those who are doing it."

Every great inventor, or innovator, had to produce their first invention against vigorous opposition.

THE TEN MOST IMPORTANT PEOPLE YOU KNOW:

1. Those who love and believe in you.
2. Those who stand by you in bad times.
3. Those you can be "natural" with.
4. Those you can be intimate with.
5. Those who challenge you.
6. Those who encourage you.
7. Those who see that your good points overshadow the bad.
8. Those who give you honest feedback.
9. Those who are sensitive to your needs.
10. Those you do not feel "obligated" to pay back.

Surround yourself with people who are important to you.

Respond to the needs of others.

A negative attitude is any attitude that blinds us to solutions and opportunities. A positive attitude is any attitude that opens our minds so that we can see them.

Create from a foundation of things that are important to you.

The only differences between a rut and a groove are the dimensions.

Even the Lone Ranger didn't ride alone.

It is by the integration of our unique talents, strengths, and interests that we are propelled forward.

To arrive there together we must be going the same direction.

Shared values are the best base for effective teamwork.

Teamwork is built on trust.

Stop trying to do it alone.

Teams reach destinations that individuals only think about.

Team goals should have deadlines.

A goal of the team is to tap the strengths of the individuals who make it up.

Each team member must feel comfortable speaking candidly to the other members of the team.

Mountain climbers must help each other reach the top.

Problems can become opportunities when the right people come together.

— ROBERT REDFORD

The future will require us to be able to work together with a very diverse work group.

None of us has the entire solution. We are all a piece of the puzzle. When a piece is missing, problems persist.

Teams can turn fragments of ideas into positive change.

The biggest block to team creativity is the voice of blame.

Teams should ask "What would we do if we knew it was impossible to fail?"

Never tell people how to do things. Tell them what to do, and they will surprise you with their ingenuity.

— GEORGE S. PATTON

Creativity flows in the direction of rewards.

To creative people the purpose of communications is understanding not agreement.

Many ideas are variations of other ideas.

People are creative when they feel challenged.

Only promote people whose greatest pleasure is bragging about the accomplishments of their team.

Combine the enthusiasm and ideals of youth with the wisdom and experience of maturity and mix them with the strengths of diversity.

The goal of creativity is not just to create new products and ideas, but also build teamwork and harmony.

Reward team as well as individual creativity.

CREATIVE ACTIONS

1. Ask someone to give you feedback on your ideas.

2. Join or create a group that is focused on creativity.

3. Solicit input on your ideas from people with a variety of viewpoints.

4. Do "joint creativity" programs.

5. Ask yourself, "Who can help me with this idea?"

6

creative courage

THINKING OUTSIDE THE BOX

The box is our comfort zone—its sides are comprised by our education, our experience, our self concept and our ability to take intelligent risks. The size and quality of our ideas will be in direct proportion to our ability to extend our thoughts beyond these self-imposed boundaries. Do it on purpose! Make a habit of it!

On the road to success, many step off before they get there.

↞ G. GORDON LIDDY

If everyone would sweep their own stoop the whole world would be clean.

↞ OLD PROVERB

If it's not illegal, immoral, or fattening . . . go for it!

Always be satisfied with your best, not with less.

Courage and creativity are usually found together.

Creativity is 1 percent inspiration and 99 percent perspiration.

↞ THOMAS EDISON

The three great requirements for a happy life:

    Something to do
    Something to love
    Something to hope for

No handicap matters if you have the idea and the heart.

If you are going to panic, at least panic intelligently.

Officially death occurs when the brain stops functioning.

If you have built castles in the air, your work need not be lost. That is where they should be. Now put foundations under them.

— HENRY DAVID THOREAU

Creativity is fundamentally an expression of who we are, not what we do or have.

The final forming of a person's character lies in their own hands.

＜ ANNE FRANK

Would-be innovators must be bold enough to dismiss the voices of fear and doubt.

Intelligent mistakes are an essential part of team growth.

Success is 80 percent creative, 20 percent planning, and 100% work.

Ultimately we know deeply that the other side of every fear is freedom.

＜ MARILYN FERGUSON

Drive out fear.

— Dr. W. Edwards Deming

Don't let your dream or vision die because of a lack of sustained effort.

Creating is being in partnership with God.

— Bernard B. Goldman, Ph.D.

Everything that is was once imagined.

— Ted Joans

Determine what you want in your life and then apply creative thinking to put it there.

The mind is not a storehouse to be filled but an instrument to be used.

— John Gardner

The harder you work, the luckier you get.

The greatest risk of all? Not to risk!

Only those who dare to fail can ever achieve greatly.

One creative thinker creates a majority.

Here's a test to find when your mission on earth is finished. If you're alive, it isn't.

— RICHARD BACH

If you want the rainbow, you gotta put up with the rain.

— DOLLY PARTON

Opportunities are usually disguised as hard work, so most people don't recognize them.

— ANN LANDERS

The world ages us too fast. We grow up too quickly, we stop dreaming too early, and we develop the ability to worry at far too young an age.

— DOUG WECKER

Anytime you try to win everything, you must be willing to lose everything.

To see what is right and not do it is lack of courage.

Creativity, plus courage, plus work equals miracles.

Courage is not failing to fall, but getting back up.

All life is a chance, but what a beautiful chance.

To accomplish something important you must be willing to stick your neck out.

Creative effort pays in more coins than cash.

Creative power needs no ivory tower.

Success must be defined in personal terms. Until you can define what success means to you, you cannot focus your creative effort on it. Think about the things that you would do if you knew it was impossible to fail. Then go out with all the fire, drive, enthusiasm, and sweat you can muster, and make it happen. The sheer joy of sustained creative effort is a bonus you will enjoy.

The best never rest. The men and women who get the most from their ideas always want to understand more about everything.

Success is a journey, not a destination.

Important goals motivate us to keep going even when failure seems inevitable.

Sticking to it is the genius.

— Thomas Edison

Age doesn't matter unless you're cheese.

Your creative engine is often lubricated by midnight oil.

What are your dreams worth? What are you willing to risk?

Success is largely the product of not giving up.

Throughout history, the most common debilitating human ailment has been "cold feet."

It is easy—terribly easy—to shake a person's faith in themselves.

— GEORGE BERNARD SHAW

There are penalties for negative attitudes.

Anxiety is the handmaiden of creativity.

— DAVID GOLEMAN

A certain level of conflict is healthy.

If you rest, you rust. Keep moving forward.

Use it or lose it.

I've never met an ugly person, only a lazy one.

→ HELENA RUBINSTEIN

It takes courage to change.

Life is too long not to do it right.

→ DIANE DEACON

People who fly into a rage always make a bad landing.

→ WILL ROGERS

Creativity is the trait that makes us human.

Ideas will fly in our windows if we've opened them.

A fool is someone whose pencil wears out before its eraser does.

— MARILYN VOS SAVANT

You must be able to trust your own mind.

Intuition is "feeling knowledge."

If you don't want to do something, one excuse is as good as another.

Success doesn't come to you . . . you go for it.

— MARVE COLLINS

Making an idea work is much more difficult than coming up with it in the first place.

Creative people are challenged rather than discouraged by challenges.

Dealing with rejection is part of the creative process.

It is the "driving force" of creativity which is so "remarkably unequal"—not the degree of native talent.

— BROOKS ATKINSON

God works with you . . . not for you.

The difficulty lies not so much in developing new ideas as in escaping from old ones.

— JOHN MAYNARD KEYNES

The truly creative person has far more opportunities in nearly every field. More people kill ideas than think them up.

Be a "go-giver" as well as a "go-getter."

— LEONARD HUDSON

Give your trouble to God; He will be up all night anyway.

Creativity is obviously not solely the product of experts.

— DIGITAL INNOVATION

Make a decision to be creative.

The difference between winning and losing is frequently not quitting.

— WALT DISNEY

Creativity is equal parts heart and mind.

If you risk nothing, you risk everything.

↜ GEENA DAVIS

You must do the thing you think you cannot do.

↜ ELEANOR ROOSEVELT

I'm not going to limit myself because people won't accept the fact that I can do something else.

↜ DOLLY PARTON

Creativity is a natural birthright for all of us. However, many of us choose not to embrace this capacity out of fear.

↜ DEENA METZGER

You can if you think you can.

— Norman Vincent Peale

It is better to attempt great things and fail than to attempt small things and succeed.

Goals and actions must meet.

Never give up!

— Sir Winston Churchill

Behind every great idea are people lined up saying "it won't work."

To commit to a life of creativity and innovation is to exercise our deepest personal values.

We can do anything we want to do if we stick to it long enough.

— HELEN KELLER

Be fearless with your creativity.

A creative spirit demands risk taking.

Don't ask for permission to be creative,
just do it!

Courage is found in action. It has to be
learned—and earned.

＞ DOUG HALL

If at first you don't succeed, you're
about average.

Courage is more exhilarating than fear,
and in the long run, it is easier.

＞ ELEANOR ROOSEVELT

Common sense is the common
denominator of intelligent people.

Everybody is ignorant, only on different
subjects.

           ⟵ WILL ROGERS

Courage makes it possible to do the
right thing when the right thing is
unpopular.

           ⟵ DAVID WECKER

Sometimes the best credential is scar
tissue formed by battling resistance to a
great idea.

Successful living requires courage.

The greatest form of courage is creative courage.

↞ ROLLO MAY

The new hero is the innovator.

↞ ALVIN TOFFLER

The Lord will not give us challenges beyond our ability. I just wish he didn't love me so much.

↞ MOTHER THERESA

Don't expect your thoughts to be "finished." Your "mental gold" must be refined just as real gold is.

If your soul yearns to live with creativity as your first priority, I can assure you that your time will come. You don't need to force it, and you certainly don't need to prove anything to anyone—except maybe yourself. When the time is right, the resolve will be there. In the meantime, you may just need to draw upon your patience.

— LYNN WEISS, PH.D.

Fewer things are sadder than looking back on your life and saying, "I wish I had . . ."

— *THE COURAGE CONNECTION*

The Four Dangers to Overcome

The Danger of Futility—The feeling or attitude that things are hopeless or a goal is unattainable.

The Danger of Expediency—The belief that long range goals and visions should bend before the immediate crisis.

The Danger of Timidity—Few people are willing to stand alone and brave the disapproval of colleagues.

The Danger of Comfort—The temptation to follow the easiest course.

These and other dangers must be overcome again and again by the creative innovator.

BULLETPROOF YOUR IDEAS

Keep the value of your ideas in focus. Where you concentrate on how creative success will benefit you and others, criticisms will bounce off the ideas as though they are bulletproof.

Courage creates confidence, confidence fuels contribution, contribution translates to success.

Don't follow a path, make new roads.

Give me a stock clerk with a dream and I will give you a person who can make history. Give me a person without a dream and I will give you a stock clerk.

— J. C. PENNEY

Both fear and noncurious conviction are blocks to your natural creativity.

— MICHAEL RAY

There are no secrets to success: Don't waste time looking for them. Success is the result of perfection, hard work, learning from failure, loyalty to those for whom you work and great persistence.

— GENERAL COLIN POWELL

Success is the peace of mind you have from knowing you have done all that you can to be all you can be.

— EARL NIGHTINGALE

CASHING IN ON YOUR CREATIVITY

1. Decide whether your creative activities are a hobby or a profession.
2. Develop the ability to repeat or initiate creative performance on demand (such as an artist or songwriter).
3. Do your creative work with enthusiasm.
4. Recognize that creative success is both fun and work. The key is to give emphasis to both.

CREATIVE ACTIONS

1. When you fear something, remind yourself of its value.

2. Say to yourself, "I can do this!"

3. Create a "courage support group."

4. When you think you are at the end of the line . . . take one more step.

5. Visualize successfully doing the thing that you fear.

7

taking the creative plunge

Take the time to imagine yourself as the creative person you want to be. This is an important step in developing your creative edge.

— WILLIAM C. MILLER

STEPS TO CREATIVE SUCCESS

1. Decide what you want to do (or be).
2. Trust your crazy ideas.
3. Act on your creative impulses.
4. Take a daily step or action toward your goal.
5. Form creative alliances.
6. Develop a checklist/timetable/plan.
7. Break routines.
8. Remind yourself of the value of your goal.
9. Visualize yourself succeeding.
10. Keep at it.
11. Have fun.
12. Keep growing and learning.
13. Develop courage connections.
14. Expose your idea to people who can help you.
15. Don't give up.

THE TEN MOST COMMON OBSTACLES TO CREATIVE SUCCESS

10. Lack of time allocated to develop and think about your idea.

9. Failure to secure a good base of creative support.

8. Not allocating enough resources to turn the idea into reality.

7. Not really knowing "how" to develop and market.

6. Being too protective about your ideas. People need to know about your idea before they can help you.

5. Not having a large enough market to support your idea.

4. Neglecting certain aspects of idea development and marketing because you don't like to do it.

3. Presenting your idea in such a way that there is a lack of perceived value.

2. Failing to use creativity to sell and promote the idea.

1. Not believing in the idea, the project or yourself.

Number one may surprise you, but you must believe in yourself and your idea before others will. Your passion and enthusiasm are vital aspects of a successful effort.

The use of positive affirmations plants positive thoughts in our subconscious. From the subconscious, creativity flows.

CRE-ATTITUDES: ATTITUDES THAT PROMOTE CREATIVITY

1. I will trust my crazy ideas.
2. I will doubt my doubts.
3. I believe the sky is not the limit.
4. I know that the power of imagination is limitless.
5. I listen to my inner voice.
6. I capture my ideas.
7. I form new associations.
8. I keep feeding my mind and senses.

 9. I create in areas that I am passionate about.

10. I choose to be creative.

11. I accept failure and mistakes as essential steps toward success.

12. I prefer "creative clutter" to "sterile neatness."

13. I commit to the "work of creativity" and not just the "fun of it."

14. I choose to light a candle rather than curse the darkness.

15. I believe in my own creativity and nurture creativity in others.

Review these affirmations. Let them sink into your subconscious. They will serve you well.

THE IDEA BANK

One of the easiest and most effective ways to capture your ideas is to keep an idea bank. A journal or three-by-five-inch cards are both excellent methods. Your computer can also help, but you don't always have your computer with you.

Review your ideas at least once a week. Write down comments or additional insights you get about your ideas. It will help synthesize your thoughts. Ideas are always a work in progress.

Combine the enthusiasm and ideals of youth with the wisdom and experience of maturity and mix them with the strengths of diversity.

GOOD IDEA?

Is it doable?

Is the timing right?

Is the risk worth it?

Is it better than now exists?

Is it people compatible?

Is the market big enough?

Is this something I really care about?

If you decide that the idea is something that is important to you and can help people, the odds of success are overwhelmingly in your favor.

Emotion is the creative power of the mind.

> ← DR. RAYMOND CHARLES BARKER

Creativity is the natural order of life.

> ← JULIA CAMERON

Creative power is inexhaustible.

Think and act like a creative person and you will become one.

March to the beat of your own drummer.

> ← HENRY DAVID THOREAU

An idea in a cage is like a silver dollar buried in the ground. Both are safe, but neither produces anything.

> ← DR. MYRON S. ALLEN

Keep raising your creative ceiling.

The more vividly you can imagine the results of your creative efforts before you begin creating them, the more likely you'll be able to complete what you start.

— C. DIANE EALY, PH.D.

If we want to change the world, we must first change ourselves.

Creativity should be treated as a skill. Like any other skill it can be improved with practice.

Listen to your heart as well as your mind.

The idea is like a blueprint; it creates an image of the form, which then magnetizes and guides the physical energy to flow into that form and eventually manifests it on the physical plane.

— SHAKTI GAWAIN

The dictionary is the only place where success comes before work.

— ARTHUR BRISBANE

Externalizing your thoughts on paper will help creativity flow.

Ideas have to be combined and messed with before they work well.

— ROGER DOW

When you find something interesting, drop everything else and study it.

— B. F. SKINNER

Get a good idea and stay with it.

— WALT DISNEY

The most creative ideas come when people say the first thing that comes into their heads.

— JOHN CLEESE

Get started . . . and keep going.

Enjoy the creative ride. If you don't enjoy the ride, you probably won't enjoy the rewards either.

You cannot build a reputation on what you intend to do.

— LIZ SMITH

The ultimate prison we need fear is our inertia and indecision.

Perhaps creativity is not in the answers but in the questions we ask.

Be surprised by something every day.

The quieter you become, the more you can hear.

Act as if it were impossible to fail.

━ DOROTHEA BRANDE

Your life will be an accumulation of your actions. The actions that you take will be a reflection of your thoughts.

Chart the steps needed to turn your ideas into reality. Include a timeline and a budget. If you can't put it on a sheet of paper, you probably can't do it . . . and vice versa.

Pursue your idea in your spare time until you are earning more from your idea than your "day job."

Our ideas will work if we do!

Criticism is the easiest form of intellectual activity.

Whatever you can do or dream you can, begin it. Boldness has genius, power, and magic in it.

— GOETHE

I not only use all the brains I have, but all I can borrow.

— WOODROW WILSON

The surest way to fail is to sit around waiting for a break.

To create you must quiet your mind. You need a quiet mind so that ideas will have the chance of connecting.

> — ERIC MAISIL, PH.D.

Tradition is a guide, not a jailer. A new attitude invariably creates a new result.

Testing an idea by actual application is the surest form of evaluation.

Affirmation: Every day in every way I'm getting better and better.

> — EMILE COUE

Fertile ground for new ideas is the idea "junkyard." Many ideas that failed did so due to poor execution, not because of the value of the idea itself.

People who notice details most of us miss are more creative.

All new ideas seem wild at first.

Set aside time to think. Time spent thinking will improve the results of "doing."

True creativity is impossible without some measure of passion.

Make a daily inventory of your blessings.

Look in the mirror every morning and say "Yes, I Can!"

Don't fall prey to the paralysis of analysis.

A creative spirit first and foremost requires curiosity.

— JORDAN AYAN

An ounce of ideas is worth a pound of information.

— GERALD HAMAN

Creativity is behavior as well as thought.

Every day take a step toward your dream. No matter how small that step is, it builds a momentum that attracts resources and greatly increases the odds of success.

It's the start that stops most people.

Change is inevitable except from a vending machine.

A candle loses nothing by lighting another candle.

— JAMES KELLER

Don't be a has-been. Be a will-be.

— LAUREN BACALL

OPEN MIND SURGERY

An open mind is the beginning of growth and progress. It makes us receptive to new information, ideas, and concepts that can be synergized with others.

Never argue with your barber until after he finishes styling your hair.

— RONNIE WILKINS

Stretch your mind.
Ask "Why not?"
     "What if?"
     "Couldn't we?"

CREATIVE ACTIONS

1. When you begin, don't second-guess yourself.

2. When you plunge, do it wholeheartedly.

3. Ask yourself, "When is the right time to do this?"

4. Make the plunge without a safety net other than trusting your ability.

5. Remind yourself that without taking the plunge, your life will stay the same.

8

thinking the unthinkable

Never cry over spilled milk. Invent a better milk carton.

— JACK FOSTER

"What would you do if you knew it was impossible to fail?" is still one of the great questions we can ask ourselves.

People who are creative see not only what actually exists, but what could.

Compared to what we might be, we are only half awake.

— WILLIAM JAMES

Dream up the biggest dream that you possibly can, in the area in which you are the most capable of making an impact.

Chances are, the more puzzled looks your idea creates, the better your idea is.

↞ UNITED TECHNOLOGIES

Do not follow where the path may lead. Go instead where there is no path and leave a trail.

Revolutionary Thinking

1. *Purge*—Dispose of old prejudices, procedures and presuppositions that could and do constrict your thinking.
2. *Prod*—Attack challenges in ways that force you to consider new solutions and new courses of action.
3. *Precipitate*—All of a sudden, out of nowhere, out drops something wild because we're thinking differently.

—Guy Kawasaki

What is now proven was once only imagined.

—WILLIAM BLAKE

The single most valuable and underutilized resource is creativity.

Anything the mind can conceive and believe, it can achieve.

—DR. NORMAN VINCENT PEALE

Our ideals are our possibilities.

— WILFERD PETERSON

If you are not living on the edge, you are taking up too much space.

— LOU WHITAKER

Imagination is the highest kite one can fly.

— LAUREN BACALL

To change your results you must change your thoughts.

Doubt your doubts.

           — JOE BATTEN

When we create something, we always create it first in thought form.

           — SHAKTI GAWAIN

Become as little children. . . .

           — JESUS

"Imagineering" means "let your imagination soar and then engineer it down to earth."

           — ALCOA

Disney now has an Imagineering department.

Imagination is more important than knowledge.

— ALBERT EINSTEIN

Keeping your mind open in the face of uncertainty is the single most powerful secret of unleashing your creative potential.

— MICHAEL GELB

Nothing is too good to be true.

Anything one person can imagine, others can make real.

— JULES VERNE

In every work of genius, we recognize our own rejected thoughts.

— RALPH WALDO EMERSON

Few people would be able to invent the wheel if it hadn't already been invented.

↜ EDWARD DE BONO

Challenge your assumptions.

Once you get rid of preconceived notions, ideas can start to cross-pollinate.

↜ ERIC SCHULZ

The sky is no longer the limit . . . the limit is the height and breadth of our imagination.

THE LITTLE BOOK OF BIG IDEAS

You are gifted with virtually unlimited potential for learning and creativity.

— Michael Gelb

Know the limits of your expertise and get help when you need it.

Think globally.

Lofty aspirations encourage inspired effort.

An idea is a terrible thing to waste.

Anyone with a new idea is a crank—
until the idea succeeds.

— MARK TWAIN

Make a habit out of generating many
ideas and options. Usually getting an
idea that we think will work stops us
from considering alternative ideas.

Creative people have learned "how to
think" rather than "what to think."

The creative process has had more
impact, power, influence, and success
than any other process in history.

— ROBERT FRITZ

An important ability for all creators is being able to live with the unknown.

Creativity and innovation flow from a mind that is free and uninhibited.

You are remembered for all the rules you break.

— DOUGLAS MACARTHUR

Think backwards.

Many creative people suffer from artificially low creative ceilings caused by what we have been told about ourselves.

⤙ THE ARTIST'S WAY

Think like Nature. Ask "How would Nature solve this problem?"

⤙ JONAS SALK

I have a dream.

⤙ MARTIN LUTHER KING JR.

Lack of innovation and creativity has caused more failure than lack of intelligence or ability.

Free your mind and ideas will follow.

The first step creative people take, whether or not they do it consciously, is to gain inner freedom to consider new ideas and new possibilities.

— CHARLES "CHIC" THOMPSON

Look for the best and the brightest things in life.

People today are in a rut. They're afraid to think.

— HAZEL LOUISE EMERSON HALL

There ain't no rules around here! We're trying to accomplish something!

— THOMAS EDISON

Make a habit of looking beyond the obvious.

God does not need to think. Thinking is used only to supplement inadequate knowledge.

— EDWARD DE BONO

To make a great dream come true, you must first have a great dream.

— HANS SELYE

Globally there are six billion consumers!

You can't see the good ideas behind you by looking twice as hard at what's in front of you.

— ROGER VON OECH

You can't dig a hole in a different place by digging the same hole deeper.

— EDWARD DE BONO

Always look for new associations and new applications of things.

If at first you do succeed, try to hide your astonishment.

~ LEO B. HELZEL

Inspiration is the impact of a fact on a prepared mind.

~ LOUIS PASTEUR

Once stretched by a new idea, the mind never regains its original dimensions.

~ OLIVER WENDELL HOLMES

You can always tell good thinkers by their eagerness to prove their own conclusions wrong.

Work at being different.

Apply Dr. Oakley Ray's mini-maxi concept: "Minimize problems and maximize opportunitites!"

You are never given a dream without also being given the power to make it come true.

The mark of a good idea is when you say to yourself, "Why didn't I think of that?"

The creative spirit, far from declining with age, may actually gain in strength and vigor as an older man or woman—soaring facing the prospect of imminent death—concentrates on what really matters.

—PAUL KAUFMAN

Constantly improve your ideas by adding depth, detail, and new dimensions.

Anything can happen. That's the beauty of creating.

⤙ ERNIE HARWELL

Think beyond your lifetime if you want to accomplish something truly worthwhile.

⤙ WALT DISNEY

Smile. It makes people wonder what you are thinking.

An idea is a kind of wonderful seed. It can be planted again and again, and is always ready for further use.

⤙ DR. MYRON ALLEN

Most ideas are the results of combinations.

Create dangerously.

— ALBERT CAMUS

If a person is sitting backwards on a horse, why do we assume that it is the person who is backwards and not the horse?

Breakthrough thinking requires motivation.

Learn to look at things backward, inside out, and upside down.

Always consider the opposite of the obvious answer.

Sometimes rocking the boat is better than no movement at all.

The future will be created by men and women with the courage to fly above the crowd.

Ideas can come from anywhere at any time.

All great accomplishments begin with the germ of an idea in the mind of a creative individual.

Never lose your sense of wonder.

— JOE BATTEN

Above all, try something.

— FRANKLIN D. ROOSEVELT

Nourish your big ideas.

One of the secrets of Leonardo da Vinci's unparalleled creativity is his lifelong practice of combining and connecting disparate elements to form new patterns.

The best creative ideas often come in bursts.

If people knew how hard I worked to get my mastery, it wouldn't seem wonderful at all.

— MICHELANGELO

As long as you're going to think anyway—you might as well think BIG!

— DONALD TRUMP

If at first you do succeed, try something harder.

— ANN LANDERS

Criticism is the easiest form of intellectual activity. Applied creativity is the most challenging.

CREATIVE ACTIONS

1. Think about something that you truly believe to be impossible . . . and challenge your assumptions.

2. What are three things that we thought were unachievable that we have now accomplished?

3. What makes something impossible?

4. Why do we avoid thinking about certain things?

5. Stretch your mind by thinking an "impossible thought" every day.

9

passion and profits

Dominant human desires that creativity can address:

1. Desire for money and riches
2. Improve health or reduce pain
3. Build self-confidence
4. Gain status or prestige
5. Satisfy curiosity
6. Make leisure time more enjoyable
7. Improve skills or talents
8. Create and build a business
9. The need for excitement, thrills, mystery, or romance

10. Desire to be "in style"
11. Increase comfort
12. Increase security
13. Improve appearance
14. Increase appeal to the opposite sex
15. Reduce human suffering
16. Improve relationships
17. Enhance the quality of life
18. Make more friends
19. Improve the future
20. Increase happiness

Each of the above offer great profit potential.

How to tell when your idea has "magic":

1. Your idea is all consuming.
2. You can't turn it off.
3. Other people try to steal it, or take credit for it.
4. When you describe it to someone, they immediately have thoughts or suggestions.

— DOUG HALL

3M's 11th Commandment: Never kill an idea, just deflect it.

MAKING MONEY WITH YOUR IDEAS:

1. Go with what you know.
2. Think up products and services for big markets.
3. Create things that can be patented.
4. Make your products and services user-friendly.
5. Think up things that offer the capacity for repeat sales.
6. Have others manufacture your product.
7. Have a written plan and list of action steps.
8. Make sure you have good profit margins.
9. Use your creativity to develop imaginative ways to market and distribute.
10. Pursue your idea with gusto.

Marketing Your Idea

- Look for markets that have large numbers.
- Choose markets that you can reach easily.
- Choose markets that you can reach economically.
- Consider non-traditional marketing and distribution.
- Create your own market.
- Creativity should apply to all aspects of your aspects and not just to the idea itself.

Ask "How can I make my ideas profitable?"

Only love makes life meaningful.

People were born to innovate, to invent.

— MICROSOFT

To a mouse, cheese is cheese. That's why mousetraps are effective.

Ideas are the flowers of innovation.

Minds must soar before organizations can.

In most big companies, innovation is accidentally discovered, and just as often, innovation is accidentally lost.

— KAREN STEPHENSON

Innovate or evaporate.

— JIM HIGGINS

The business world is becoming an "idea war."

The right questions precede the right answers.

If you want to make money from your idea, you must think of it as a business.

Ask "Who would want this?" "Who would pay for this?"

Accomplishment is a spiral that originates with self-reliance and a passion for work.

Creative capital has become the number one ingredient to business success.

Creative thinkers are the backbone of the future economy.

Nobody likes to work for a loser, and a poor attitude guarantees losing.

If you place more emphasis on keeping a positive attitude than making money, you will be more successful in your career and the money will take care of itself.

＞ Dr. Willis Kennedy

Money is a by-product of our thinking, our service, and our ability.

In an era of change . . . creativity and innovation are the ultimate economic weapons.

Venture capitalists will invest in well-done business plans.

Don't rush to engage attorneys and accountants.

If your funds are limited you're better off promoting rather than protecting your idea.

Where there is no market . . . create one.

Swipe from the best, then adapt.

— TOM PETERS

SELLING YOUR IDEAS

Selling your ideas requires you to focus on the value to the user, customer, or investor. You can't sell your idea on the basis of its novelty. You must show people how it will solve a problem, create an opportunity, or fill the needs or desires of people you're trying to get to purchase your product or idea.

How an idea is received makes a difference.

Before we can have innovation, we must have creativity.

— JIM HIGGINS

Energy, effort, and enthusiasm are all parts of successful creative efforts. Take care of yourself physically. Eat and exercise sensibly. Get enough rest and relaxation. Creativity and the creative life are marathons, not hundred-yard dashes.

Ask "What would people buy today if it were available?"

Many people earn much money at the price of their own individuality and sense of independence.

— ARI KIEV, M.D.

$$L + E + I + T^2 = I$$
Leadership plus Environment plus
Incentives plus Training and Teamwork
equals Innovation

            ⌐ PARTHENON INNOVATION GROUP

The worst part of success is trying to
find someone who is happy for you.

            ⌐ BETTE MIDLER

What I wanted to be when I grew up
was—in charge.

            ⌐ WILMA VAUGHT

Quantity of ideas breeds quality of
ideas.

A quality or service program without innovation is a myth.

Aim to be the best in your business rather than the biggest.

The potential for creativity is always present.

Innovative management is a strategic weapon.

The two major reasons that an entrepreneur often receives little or nothing from their invention are inexperience and poor marketing—not a lack of innovativeness.

↞ AMERICAN BAR

Create an uninhibited environment that encourages open discussion of ideas.

Creative thoughts preceed creative results.

Pray about every difficult problem.

↞ BILL MARRIOTT

Work like you don't need the money.
Love like you've never been hurt. Dance
like nobody's watching.

— RONNIE WILKINS

Innovative leaders manage as though
they have no authority. They lead by
example and by the quality of their
ideas.

Plan your work. Work your plan.

For a creation to make a difference, it
must fill a need.

To be truly creative, you have to be drunk with your idea.

To be creative, you must care.

Include "new" and "different" in your innovation strategy as well as "better" and "more."

Abandonment of the obsolete is an important phase of creative strategy.

Don't overlook the obvious.

Hold meetings in a risk-free zone where people can speak their minds without fear of criticism or ridicule.

The ultimate secret of success is hard work.

Few organizations make a real effort to utilize the creative potential of their employees.

The demand for innovation doubles with each decade.

Your ideas communicate who you are.

Creativity and innovation are always vital but rarely urgent.

The company's most urgent task is to learn to welcome, beg for, demand— innovation from everyone.

⌐ TOM PETERS

Creativity is the sudden cessation of stupidity.

⌐ DR. E. LAND

Creativity precedes innovation.

Progress depends on people knowing they'll be able to profit from their ideas.

← DEBORAH NEVILLE

Innovation is an unusual game. There are at least two winners or none.

The most successful companies and nations will be those that are willing to learn from others, and creative fusion will become a strategic tool in the era of global competition.

← SHERIDAN TATSUNO

CREATIVE ACTIONS

1. Visualize yourself with all the money you could possibly want.

2. List 5 things that you feel passionately about.

3. Ask "why" something really excites you.

4. Are there other people that share your passion? Who are they?

5. Be sure that profits are the "byproduct" of your passion rather than an end in itself.

10

creating the future
(and a few predictions)

204

THE FUTURE

The human mind and spirit will not be contained. It must not be contained if we are to discover the innovations that will enable us to live in harmony with the earth, each other, and ourselves.

In the future, we will be doing things, creating things, and accomplishing more than any of us can imagine. The synergy of innovation and its potential for progress linked with technology and information is truly without boundaries. We have the ability and resources to make the future whatever we want it to be. The challenge of focusing our creativity and its power to solve problems, create opportunity, and enrich the human condition is both a challenge and a responsibility. Solutions to crime, poverty, homelessness, terrorism, and even health related issues such as depression, violence, and the delivery of health services to all, can be dealt with effectively.

CREATIVE CHALLENGES

CHURCHES

Churches must spread their ministries in new ways to reach those who typically do not attend a church service. The outreach must get to the homeless and the mentally and spiritually malnourished. It must spread hope to those countless individuals leading lives of quiet or invisible desperation.

EDUCATION

Professional educators must get the concept of life-long learning to people of all ages. Continuous learning is now a necessity. There are many ways to help people develop life skills in addition to traditional classroom instruction. The availability of information and interaction through technology make us all world leaders.

BUSINESS

Leaders must create opportunities, products, and services that assure the basic needs of individuals and families are met. They must integrate the diverse talents of people to expand opportunities to them regardless of gender or cultural background.

GOVERNMENT

We need to develop a system of innovation to link federal, state, and local governments with the ideas and solutions that can be generated by the general population. The mental resources of our country should be utilized as one of our greatest assets and natural resources.

SOCIETY

Crime, homelessness, education, and elderly issues can be dealt with if we apply a huge dose of breakthrough thinking. Innovative goals should be should be targeted and attacked for each area.

HEALTH CARE

Cures for cancer, AIDS, and other diseases are within our grasp. Making health care affordable and accessible to everyone must be a top world innovative program priority.

✻

Teaching creativity and innovation should be a fundamental part of our educational system. A creative society would put health, happiness, and prosperity within the reach of everyone.

When President Kennedy put forth the challenge, and the declaration, to "put a man on the moon by the end of the decade," he harnessed and focused our country's imagination and attention that has rarely been seen. We must do this again, and it needs to be the norm rather than the exception. Setting creative and innovative goals every year should be an important part of the presidential platform.

✻

A system of innovation should be implemented at all government levels beginning with the federal. All citizens should have an opportunity to participate. The office should be non-partisan and encourage creative ideas to deal with national and international issues. Awards should be given to people and organizations that initiate solutions that are implemented.

✻

We must capture the creative wisdom of our senior citizens. The collective experience and insights of our peers is a vast source of untapped potential. A key to innovation is the integration of our history, the now, and the future.

❋

Professional innovators will be the backbone of our future economy. Change, breakthroughs, and new products and services exist in the minds of people before they become realities.

❋

The demand for innovation and creativity will not go away. Those individuals and organizations that recognize this and make the effort to master the skills to harness their potential will be both the heroes and the winners in the years ahead.

❋

Technology will be basic to innovation in the future. Start using the information manager to log and categorize ideas.

❋

Learn to use idea generation software.

❋

Go on the Internet and tap into the virtually limitless resources you will find there.

208 CREATIVE CAPITAL

Surely the ability of a company to innovate is the result of harnessing the creative capacity of groups and individuals. That collection of people, and their ideas, represents a very real organizational asset. More and more businesses will spend considerable time and effort nurturing and retaining this vital resource.

The ability to convert thoughts and ideas into bank deposits and positive change are the challenges of the professional innovator. Be one. We need you. We're counting on you. The quality of the future depends on you.

PREDICTIONS

Despite poor records of experts predicting the future, I feel comfortable forecasting the following events.

1. Every major corporation will have a person responsible for innovation. This will be a top executive position and the demand for these individuals will be great.

2. Innovation will evolve into a professional discipline as others like accounting, architecture, and marketing have.

3. Innovation will be stressed in all the management programs of major universities. An Innovation University will become a reality.

4. A professional society will evolve to address the needs of members of this new area of expertise.

5. Innovation consulting will become one of the fastest growing areas of opportunity, helping businesses structure themselves for success in a rapidly changing global market.

6. A high-ranking government post will be created to foster innovation on a national and international basis. Solutions to many of our greatest problems will come from ideas contributed by the general population.

7. Thinking will become a basic course in the nation's fundamental education program.

8. Health-care breakthroughs will conquer AIDS, cancer, and heart disease.

9. People will be happier, healthier, and more prosperous.

10. Because of our ability to grasp our collective creative potential, the twenty-first century will be glorious.

KILLER BE'S!

Be Brave!
Be bold!
Be adventurous!
Be courageous!
Be persistent!

Modern studies continue to prove
"Ancient Wisdom."

I think the problem of the management
of creative people is both fantastically
difficult and important.

— ABRAHAM MASLOW

May the force be with you.

— GEORGE LUCAS'S *STAR WARS* FILMS

CREATIVE INNOVATOR'S PRAYER

Lord, give me the insight and sensitivity to people and events that I might recognize the creative opportunities to serve and contribute.

Give me the ability to think and the courage to act creatively when I am in a position to solve problems, create opportunity, or enrich the human condition.

Help me find ways to use my creative gifts in collaboration with others who recognize the value of dreams, ideals, vision, and breakthrough thinking.

Remind me that creativity has the power to destroy or build, to create joy or sorrow, and to promote sickness or health.

Help me work through creative blocks, times of discouragement or fear, and the resistance that creative innovators inevitably face.

Help me to encourage others when they encounter frustration and obstacles.

Finally, help me to believe in my ideas and myself even when others may not.

Thank you for the gift of creativity and the opportunity to use it to create a better world.

Amen.

The concept of creativeness and the concept of the healthy, self-actualizing, fully human person seem to be coming closer and closer together, and may perhaps turn out to be the same thing.

— ABRAHAM MASLOW

I believe that the creativity that twisted a piece of wire into a paperclip and put erasers on pencils is great enough to create brotherhood and universal peace.

— WILFERD PETERSON

"Thinkonomics" will replace economics as we consider the future.

Health, happiness, and prosperity begin as a state of mind.

COMMITMENT TO MYSELF

I _____ on _____
       NAME   DATE
commit myself to a creative lifestyle. I will set creative goals for myself and take a step every day toward their accomplishment.

_____
                        SIGNATURE

Most of my ideas belonged to other people who didn't bother to develop them.

↞ Thomas Edison

The single most valuable and underutilized resource is creativity.

Great ideas need landing gear as well as wings.

↞ C. D. Jackson

Creativity is what makes life worth living.

We are the first generation that has the information, technology, communications, resources, and imagination to create the future. The question becomes, Do we have the will and desire to do so?

Real creativity is not in the answers, but in the questions we ask.

Happiness is worth the effort.

Treat ideas (and idea people) with respect. They are our future.

We need to make the world safe for the creativity and intuition that will make the world safe for us.

         — EDGAR MITCHELL, *APOLLO* ASTRONAUT

The best way to predict your future is to create it.

THE LITTLE BOOK OF BIG IDEAS

216 Our mind is the most valuable possession that we have. The quality of our lives is, and always will be, a reflection of how well we develop, train, and utilize this precious gift. The only "real" limitation on our future is our ability to harness our mental resources. Tapping the wealth and the potential of our minds is the last professional frontier.

You have a creative contribution to make. Your life, and mine, will be better if you do.

— MICHAEL TOMS

The greatest secret of success in life is for a person to be ready when their opportunity comes.

— BENJAMIN DISRAELI

It is never too late to be what you might have been.

The greatest force in the world is the power of applied thought.

The world that you live in will be a living expression of how you are, have and will use your mind.

Make sure that people see the big picture.

Leaders must infect their firms with the growth attitude.

Creativity is for everyone. Each of us has something creative to contribute, no matter what the task. It is up to us to take up the baton and manifest our own creative symphony through whatever task we find meaningful.

— MICHAEL TOMS

Whatever is wrong ought to be fixed.

The future never just happened. It was created.

⌁ WILL & ARIEL DURANT

In our time, the creative mind is in jeopardy.

⌁ NORMAN COUSINS

A future based on creativity is bright.

⌁ JOHN KAO

You can go anywhere with a dream and a #2 pencil.

Where minds are open, there will always be a frontier.

History is essentially a serial of ideas.

— ALEX OSBORN

The time has come to do for innovations what we first did for management in general . . . create the principle, the tasks and the discipline.

— DR. PETER F. DRUCKER

Creative work should enable a person to reach their potential.

Different is not always better, but better is always different.

Bad things usually happen on their own. Good things we have to make happen.

The world hungers for positive attitudes.

A creative attitude is the fuel of progress and growth.

Executives have up to 1,000 hours of management training and less than 10 hours in innovations and creativity training.

— TONY BUZAN

Every person with a positive attitude is a beacon of hope.

The future is no longer an extension of the past.

In the cultivation of creative power lies the greatest hope for a better world.

Use innovation to make the world smile.

Creativity is God's gift to us. Using creativity is our gift back to God.

— JULIA CAMERON

The future is that time when you'll wish you'd done what you aren't doing now.

You can't build the future in the future.

Thought inspired by love will yet rule the world.

The demands of our creative abilities have doubled in every generation.

— DR. PETER F. DRUCKER

There is always a better way—our challenge is to find it.

Anything not creating is decaying or dying.

Our destiny is not in the stars but in our creative minds.

HEALTH

Dr. Oakley Ray of Vanderbilt University has researched the mind-body link with dramatic results. He explained that thoughts that can make us sick also have the potential to promote health. Creative thinking may be the best "fountain of youth" that is available to us. Exercising our mental muscles is surely as important as lifting weights or jogging. The combination of proper diet, exercise, and thinking will add not only years to our life, but life to our years.

It's not the critic who counts.

— THEODORE ROOSEVELT

The important thing is this: to be able at any moment to sacrifice what we are for what we could become.

— CHARLES DuBois

Creative thinking promotes health and hope. When we create our future, we feel good about ourselves.

Once you've opened your brain and realized your potential, you'll never be satisfied with mindless mediocrity.

— DOUG HALL

Creativity can solve any problem.

— GEORGE LOIS

There is no doubt about it—ideas
change history.

— FRANK GOBLE

The religion of the future will be a
bouquet of the great truths of all the
religions of the world, tied with the
golden cord of love.

— WILFERD PETERSON

The "what if" question begs for
completion: "What if we tried. . . ?"

— DALE DAUTEN

A single idea can transform a life, a
business, a nation, a world.

226 Put your interest in the future because you are going to be spend the rest of your life there.

Make the world smile with creativity and innovation.

Sometimes by the time we have the answer, the questions have changed.

There's no use running when you are on the wrong road.

Each new year brings 365 days of opportunity.

Human history is, in essence, a history of ideas.

— H. G. WELLS

WHY NOT?

What if we had an Office of Creativity and Innovation as part of the Federal Government (or State and Local)? Social issues could be presented to the national population. People of all ages, backgrounds, and nationalities could present their creative ideas to a "non-political" department that would evaluate them and steer them to the appropriate resource for action. Public incentives and awards could be provided. Schools and churches could take on projects.

Creativity and innovation are to the information age what iron and coal were to the industrial age.

There is no power like the power of an idea whose time has come.

A flow of good ideas can keep the good times from turning bad.

— MARION BUHAGAIR

Great thoughts precede great results. Want to change your life? Change your thoughts.

The power of ideals is incalculable.

The only aging process is the erosion (rather than the pursuit) of our ideals.

Solutions and profits are only ideas away.

Try not. Do. Or do not. There is no try.

— YODA

To stay ahead, you must have your next idea waiting in the wings.

— ROSABETH MOSS KANTER

Creativity is the cause. Progress is the effect.

Creativity cannot be ordered like breakfast at the Waldorf. Instead it must be stimulated, motivated and induced.

— ROY ASH

Expect the best.

— JOE BATTEN

The innovator has for enemies all who have done well under the old, and lukewarm defenders in those who may do well under the new.

— MACHIAVELLI, 1513

In the next twenty years, the commerce of ideas is going to become more important than the commerce of things.

— DOUGLAS VAN HOUWELING

To raise new questions, new possibilities,
to regard old problems from a new angle,
requires creative imagination.

— ALBERT EINSTEIN

The creative process is an exploration
that is never finished—a journey that
never ends.

By the time I had the answers, they
changed the questions.

The human race is governed by its
imagination.

— NAPOLEON BONAPARTE

Creativity can solve any problem.

— GEORGE LOIS

Remember, innovation is God's way of short-circuiting the status quo.

Creativity and innovation are required because today's issues have no precedent.

Keep your creativity goal directed.

Bringing out your own unique brand of creativity into your life and the world can be the most significant thing you'll ever do.

— LORNA CATFORD, PH.D.

Rapidly occurring changes in today's world and workplace are creating great opportunities for individuals and organizations that have the capacity to innovate.

A creative vision allows you to operate and live proactively.

Being powerful is like being a lady. If you have to tell people you are, you are not.

           ← MARGARET THATCHER

Great things require great passion and great effort.

Use changes as a fuel for opportunity.

Our greatest strength is mind power.

Progress is achieved by the progressive realization of creative goals.

We need to find God, and He cannot be found in noise and restlessness.

          — MOTHER THERESA

The capacity to create is unlimited.

The only real aging process is the erosion of our ideals.

          — ALBERT SCHWEITZER

Accelerating change and increasing complexity multiply the value of intellectual capital.

The age of nations is past. The challenge now is to build the earth.

          — TEILHARD deCHARDIN

Think!

—Thomas Watson Jr.

There is more to life than increasing its speed.

—Mahatma Gandhi

Use your creative gifts.

The future will not be a gift. It will be an achievement.

Beware when the great God lets loose a thinker on this planet.

—Ralph Waldo Emerson

How can you tell a creative person?
They create things. Be one! Do it!

By their fruits you will know them.

— THE BIBLE

The future is never here.

If you and I exchange a penny, we both
may still only have one penny. But, if we
exchange ideas, you have two ideas and I
have two ideas.

Live your life so that your children can
tell their children that you not only stand
for something wonderful—you acted on
it.

— DAN ZADRA

GLOBAL CREATIVITY

The internet, satellites, new technology, creative educated men and women, information systems, materials, speed and many other features of today's social and professional environment make it possible to integrate creative efforts as never before. Setting global creative goals can become a practical challenge for innovative leaders. The "how to" is difficult but doable. Let's be the generation that begins the process.

Next year at this time you will wish you had started today things that you now wish you had started a year ago. Think about it!

CREATIVE ACTIONS

1. What are the contributions that you want to make to the future?

2. What would you pursue if you knew that success was a sure thing?

3. What will be the greatest thing about the future?

4. What do you want your legacy to be?

5. Don't "save" your creative ability, "spend it."

SUMMARY

Our future is about creative thinking and innovative action. Now that you have reviewed these ideas, thoughts and strategies, put them to your personal use. Think about them, talk about them and implement them into the fabric of your organization . . . and your life. You'll be glad you did.

Give this book to a friend and encourage them to do the same. Be a link in the creative chain that puts health, happiness and prosperity within the reach of everyone.

For information on the products and services of Parthenon Innovation Group or to become a Certified Professional Innovator:

    Call: (615) 329-4849
    Or write: Parthenon Innovation Group
            Suite 316
            1719 West End Avenue
            Nashville TN 37023

ABOUT THE AUTHOR

Harold McAlindon is an award-winning speaker, consultant, and business executive. The developer of the CIP (Certified Professional Innovator) Program and the author of numerous articles and books on innovation, creativity, and human potential, he is the president of Parthenon Innovation Group in Nashville, Tennessee.